FIRST AND ONLY

Powering Up Your Mindset for Transplant and Living Sickle Cell Free

Adewale J. Lawal

10-10-10
Publishing

FIRST AND ONLY
www.firstandonlynow.com

Copyright © 2019 Adewale J. Lawal

ISBN: 978-1088409152

Publisher
10-10-10 Publishing
Markham, ON   Canada

Printed in Canada and the United States of America

Table of Contents

Dedicated to my mother
the one and only Mrs. Taiwo O. Lawal
widow, mother, and friend

Dear Mummy,
I dedicate this book to you. I am the man that I am today because
you always taught me how to stay positive, work hard, and be an
honest, helpful, selfless human being.

I Learned from You

I learned about love from you,
Watching your caring ways.
I learned about joy from you
In fun-filled yesterdays.
From you I learned forgiving
Of faults both big and small.
I learned what I know about living
From you, as you gave life your all.
The example you set is still with me;
I'd never want any other.
I'm thankful for all that you taught me,
And I'm blessed to call you "Mother."

– Joanna Fuchs

Acknowledgements

I would like to thank my loving wife, who has supported me in sickness and in health for many years without complaint. She has driven me to be the best I could be. She is now part of my soul.

Thank you, Mother, for raising me the way you did. Thank you for the morals you instilled in me, and the endless love, guidance, patience, and admiration you have given me. I would not be the person I am today without you.

Also, my sisters and brothers need to be mentioned as they have also supported me and advised me. A special acknowledgement goes out to my brother, Gbenga, without whom I may not be here. Thank you for being my friend and donor.

I would also like to thank my doctors, Dr. Besser and Dr. Potter, and all the nurses that have looked after me in the past four years at Addenbrooke's and Kings College Hospitals. You have been great.

I must thank the congregation of Ely Cathedral. Thank you for your kindness, love, and support in the darkest hours; and a big thank you to Canon Victoria Johnson, Dean, and the Very Revd. Mark Bonney, for their help and support when I was sick.

A big acknowledgement and thank you to my friends—Suzanne, Paul, Paul, Carol, Kevin, Neal, Kevin, and Steve—for just being there when I needed to talk to someone or ask for advice. You are the best friends anyone could ask for. I would also like to thank Toby Bakare and Victoria MacDonald for their help and assistance when I needed them.

First and Only

I thank Mr. Raymond Aaron, *New York Times* Top 10 best-selling author, and friend, who has provided me with a wealth of knowledge, and has advised and inspired me in so many positive ways.

There are many more people I could thank, but time, space, and modesty compel me to stop here.

Adewale
25 July 2019

About the Author

Adewale Lawal, author of *First and Only*, is also the author of *Creative Endeavour for the Logical Mind*, and is a Chartered Mechanical Engineer and Masters graduate of Surrey University. He carved out a career in manufacturing before starting his own successful business as a manufacturing consultant, providing incisive and expert advice to some of the world's leading blue-chip companies.

Following a prolonged period of ill health, all this changed for Adewale. He decided to explore ways to build an online business, soon finding himself in the realms of online marketing, and discovering a whole new discipline and language, at the polar opposite of the more familiar engineering world. Realising there was a method, process, and system in this new world, the intricacies of online marketing began to gradually unravel. Recognising how sophisticated building an online business can be, Adewale invested heavily in his education, and committed to learning and masterminding from the best in the industry, who have achieved success in this field.

Adewale lives in Cambridgeshire with his wife, Julie, who shares his newfound passion for marketing, building online businesses, and helping other people make the same transformational life changes.

You can contact him at www.firstandonlynow.com for more information and to book a consultation.

Foreword

This book is written by a young at heart man who has overcome a major life-changing illness in his life. *First and Only* is written by Mechanical Engineer turned Entrepreneur and online marketer, Adewale Lawal. In this book, Adewale unravels the startling illnesses he had to overcome, his fight to get treated, the miracle treatment and how he amazingly overcame his illnesses.

As a successful business owner for many years providing manufacturing consultancy to blue-chip companies, Adewale always enjoyed helping clients achieve the breakthroughs needed to solve complex business problems. In this edition, Adewale has applied the same methodical thinking to break down his key success strategies into digestible sections.

This is an inspirational journey; struck by serious health issues, Adewale's story is a classic hero overcoming adversity story. This is truly breathtaking. On the road to recovery with renewed focus, Adewale started to explore alternative options to build an online business. He has developed new courses to help individual entrepreneurs realise their Why and build their mindset for success.

This is one remarkable man's journey of never giving up in the face of adversity, staying focused and keeping the momentum going during the astonishing cycle of challenges and successes, from Engineer to Entrepreneur.

Raymond Aaron
New York Times Bestselling Author

Part 1

Growing up and Living with Sickle Cell Anaemia

Chapter 1

My Attitude Toward You Will Always Reflect Your Attitude Toward Me

The Young Me

One of my first memories was of going to school in Nigeria, in a white Mercedes limo. When I was little, we travelled around quite often. I was born in Wellington, India, as my father was posted there in the Nigerian Navy, to study and further educate himself in Material Science. We travelled a lot at first, and then we went home to Nigeria.

At the age of around four to six, when I was in Nigeria, I was sick a lot, and my doctor suspected that I had sickle cell anaemia. It wasn't until I was six years old that I came to the UK and was formally diagnosed at Kings College Hospital in London.

It was a year later when my parents asked me if I wanted to go to school in the UK, with my sisters. I said yes, and the next thing I knew, I was packing my bags and moving to a boarding school in Bristol. It was nowhere near my sisters, as I was in the West of England, and they were up near Cambridge, in the East of England. The reason for this was that my father was Admiral of the Nigerian Navy, and Governor of Lagos State.

It was tough for me at first, because the winter was so cold; in fact, it snowed heavily that year. This was a shock, having come from a sweltering 32°C, to minus 2°C. I ended up with chilblains, and suffered

3

terribly from the cold. As a seven-year-old, I had to wear shorts as part of my school uniform, and this made it even worse. I got to make a few friends, however, who became my friends throughout school, and we all suffered together.

A big problem with boarding school is that you have to fight for survival. And the best way to do that is to pick a fight with the biggest person there is, even though you don't stand any chance whatsoever. This is guaranteed to get you beaten up, but hopefully not put you in hospital. However, the plus side is that people will think you are crazy enough not to be messed with. Therefore, they will leave you alone for the time you are in the school. This plan worked for me, and I was never challenged to another fight whilst I was at school.

As I grew up at boarding school, I began to realise that I in fact had a stubborn streak, to the point where people said that I was tenacious. For example, when the school said I couldn't do maths, physics, and chemistry O-levels, I spoke to my mother, who got me a tutor during the holidays, and they taught me the subjects. By the time the examinations came, I took maths, physics, and chemistry, and passed all of them. I also took the CSE level subjects, and I passed those too. This taught me a valuable lesson: Teachers are not always 100% right.

To be honest, I didn't always like this school. It had the traditional, strange habits of boarding schools, like the cold showers and baths when it's your birthday, or polishing your shoes at 6:30 AM, and the use of brutality to settle all your issues.

To start with, I just coped, because my cousin was at the same school. However, he was only there for my first year, and then he left suddenly—and then it became the school of 400 white kids, with just one black kid. Although everything was okay, I did have a problem every year with the same nasty little bully that I had to deal with. He would always come up to me, and he would make some abusive racist comment; and I would be forced to retaliate by punching him as hard as I could in the face, and then I would walk away. This cycle went on for 3 or 4 years before it finally stopped.

Other than those unfortunate occasions, I rarely got into any trouble whatsoever.

I remember the setup while going to boarding school: I had to have a guardian for day-to-day needs and half terms; Christmas was always spent back in Nigeria; summer was always spent in London with my mum, until she took us on holiday in some other country, like France, Italy, or Spain; and Easter would almost always be spent with another guardian, somewhere in the south, like Brighton. These were very odd times. I remember spending one Easter holiday with a lady on the South Coast, who always insisted on my sisters and me getting out of her house at 3 pm every day, to go for a walk down on the pier—and she insisted that we not return before 4 pm. We assumed that we needed to get some fresh air daily, but this was not explained in any way. She also was obsessed with showing people magazines that her daughter was in.

I also remember a kind lady in Richmond, who taught us all we needed to know about etiquette and manners. I particularly enjoyed staying in her house, as she liked me. These were bizarre holidays, and I don't really remember all of them, but they had an impact on how I grew up, and on the things I learnt outside school.

I think that by growing up mostly on my own in boarding school and in technical college, it really forced me to grow up quickly and take responsibility for my own actions. I know things would have been different if my father was still alive, but the situation could not be helped. It made me learn how to cope fast, and learn quickly, and be more resilient in every way.

Tenacity

Like I said before, I have always been tenacious. Another example of this was when it came to doing A-levels. Again, I wanted to do maths, physics, and chemistry A-levels—the sciences basically—but my school thought differently. The careers advice they gave me was to become a landscape gardener. This was totally impractical. As a sickle-cell anaemia sufferer, outdoor jobs are not advisable because of the adverse change in weather, from hot to cold and to severely cold. The thing I didn't like was that they called my mother to come to the school. She travelled all the way from Nigeria to hear this pitiful story of how I didn't have the mental aptitude to do maths, physics, and chemistry. She seemed unamused to have been dragged all this way to hear this. They could have called, or waited until she was in the country.

My mother asked me what I wanted to do, and I said I would go to a technical college and do a BTEC in mechanical engineering. So, she told the school that I was leaving. They were very shocked because they didn't expect that answer, as they thought they had complete control. However, I left the school, went on to do my BTEC in mechanical engineering, and walked away with a high distinction.

Applying to University

Now, okay then, next obstacle: I had to choose which university I was going to go to. I chose three of the top four universities for mechanical engineering. However, when I went to the first one, I was told, "We don't take BTEC students—it's the maths, you see; it is very hard." They said this to me around five times, and it made me feel unwelcome. However, they did send me a conditional offer of an average grade of 90%. The second university said, "Maths is very hard compared to BTEC; it needs you to do a lot of work—are you prepared to do so?" I said yes, and that was it; they made me an offer of 80% across-the-board.

I achieved a distinction of 94% and wrote back to the first university, declining my place, saying that although I had reached their offer, I would not go to their university because of the way I was treated throughout the interview process.

This turned out to be a continuous trend all my life because I always speak out when I see any injustice, or or when I see something wrong with the way people are treated. I always believe that people should get a fair chance in life, whether outside work or not, and I've always believed that people should be trained as much as they are interested in training. That means that if they want to know more, I am willing to teach them more.

Managing My Sickle Cell Anaemia

When I came to this country, I used to have to go to Kings College hospital once a year for a check-up, until I got to the age of about 16 or 17. I rarely had any big illnesses, as I was taken good care of by the school nurses, and they tried to advise me on what to do and what not to do.

This was okay, until my curiosity got the better of me. I began experimenting with things I was advised not to do.

I would train extensively in the gym, until my heart rate was between 170 and 190. Then I would bring it down slowly with a proper warm down. I also started playing rugby, and I found that as long as I didn't overexert myself, I was okay. This went against everything I had been taught about never exercising or exerting yourself, as that might trigger a sickle cell crisis. I tended to take things at face value, and if they didn't cause a crisis, I would continue to do them. After all, I found that when playing rugby, you end up having the backing of at least 14 other people, on and off the field, when you get in a pickle. That was also the case at university, and as I stopped playing, I became a passionate supporter instead.

This continued in university, and I lived life to the maximum of my ability—playing hard, working very hard, and exercising to the max. However, the adverse effects happened, and I was unlucky enough to catch pneumonia, several chest infections, and several sickle crises that put me out of action. In total, I spent 8 of the first 20 weeks of university life in hospital. So, it was no surprise when the university asked me to repeat my first year.

Looking back on things, it was probably the best thing that could happen, because I happened to join a group of friends that looked after one another and taught each other everything they knew, to pass the exams on all topics. That was despite coming out of hospital one week before my final exams; I had to be brought up to speed very quickly. They always encouraged me and spurred me on to success.

The next time I got really sick enough to be hospitalised was when I was in my second job, working all hours, and I couldn't see it myself, but I was highly stressed. I ended up having a crisis, and before I knew it, I was hospitalised. I was ordered to take things easy for a couple of weeks, so I quit my job, reconnected with some friends, and got a new job.

After this shock, I dared not have any more major crises for a few more years, and I did everything I could to avoid this. I did have some niggling pains in my legs, but I have managed these pains.

How, you ask? Well, over the years, I have taken many analgesics, such as diamorphine, pethidine, Tramadol, codeine, etc. I had great doctors who trusted me with these kinds of drugs, and they would check, once a year, that I wasn't getting addicted to any of them. I found that as long as I followed the prescribed amount within the allocated times, I had no problems managing the pains. There were the odd times when I had to go to hospital at two o'clock in the morning, and head to the haematology ward, to see the doctor on duty there, to ask for some stronger pain killers, but this was very rare.

My bosses throughout my career were always very understanding and helpful, with the exception of one. They were willing to make any adjustments, and were accommodating when I needed to go to hospital, or anything else.

There was one boss who actually threatened me and gave me a written warning for not telling her that I was in hospital on the weekend. I just took it and warned her that it wouldn't stand up in a court of law, as that was illegal practice in the eyes of the law. She went on to call her boss, to tell him that I was giving her lip. I said the same thing to him and then handed the phone back to her and went back to my desk. I never heard anything more about it. The point was, I wasn't about to let anybody push me about or bully me in the workplace—nor should you.

Life at University

Like I said, it wasn't really until I got to university that I got really sick, and I had a series of major crises.

I had been looking forward to going to university, although I was a little apprehensive. In the first year, I settled in, made some really nice friends, and got on with life. I was not like most students who haven't been away from home before, going on excessive rampages of binge drinking and partying. I was calmer, but I was highly stressed because the work proved to be seriously difficult.

When winter came, I got sick with chest infections, and that triggered a major crisis at three in the morning, and I had to go to the nurse, who called an ambulance to take me to hospital. They put me on a drip to get some fluids into me, and gave me a series of pethidine injections into my IV drip. This calmed me down and stopped the pain, and I slept for hours at a time. This was repeated every four to six hours for three days, and then slowly reduced until I was well enough to be discharged.

This was a regular occurrence in my first year, and I ended up missing eight out of the first thirty weeks. Because of this, I was asked to repeat the year. As I mentioned, it turned out to be a good thing, as the people in that year looked after each other more, and the friends I made would rally around when times were tough. For example, we would all have one topic, which we would learn really well, and then we would teach the others that topic.

However, in the fourth year, I ended up in hospital just before my final examinations. I came out of hospital one week before the exams, so they all rallied round to teach me everything I needed to know in order to pass each exam. I was sincerely grateful for that, and was privileged to call them my friends.

Despite this, I had a lot of fun in university, and I learnt a lot about life and friendship—including the fact that there are people out there that pretend to be your friend but secretly mean you harm. They talk about you behind your back, and bad mouth you to anyone that will listen to them; but they deny everything to your face, even when you show them proof. I had a problem with this, because of somebody's insecurities and jealousy. I ended up threatening him with pain and cutting him out of my life. I told people that they could believe what they like about me, but they would be the ones that would end up looking stupid in the end. To my recollection, there was no reason for this behaviour, except that he got a bout of the *green-eyed monster.*

I grew strong mentally and physically, and came out of university with a handful of really good friends that I could trust, whom I know will be there when I need them.

Loved Ones

My family had always been close, especially after the premature death of my father, in 1980. Everybody rallied around my mother and her children, to see what they could do for her. Eventually, they drifted apart, except my uncle (my mother's brother), who stayed around, doing everything that she needed to be done. I was also very close to my sisters when we were growing up, as I followed them around everywhere.

I drifted away from them, and others, while I was at school, and then when my little brothers came to England to go to school, I reconnected with them and looked after them. They became my responsibility in the UK, as my sisters had drifted away to the USA. I made sure that they were comfortable in their schools, and I even went to their parents evenings. I even made sure they got into university and were happy. At times, we lived together. In the end, I had to leave London to work at Johnson Matthey, in Royston, and had to leave them behind in my old flat.

My family always spoke to each other at least once a week, or even more when someone had a problem or something was wrong, but that time reduced as we got older.

Eventually, there comes a time in life when one should get married. I hit that time and beyond, to the point where I was constantly being asked when I was going to settle down and get married. I decided, in my forties, to put myself out there and start dating again. Things didn't start well as there were some strange people out there. It was my last chance. I went to a dinner-dance, and I met a lovely lady. She was just my type, and we got on so well. Eventually, we started dating. I took her to places around Cambridge, Proms in the Park, etc. It was going so well that I decided to propose to her, on the Orient Express, to Bristol from London Victoria.

We got married a little later on, at Ely Cathedral, with all the family on both sides, with my best man being Paul, the husband of the woman I consider my best friend. It was a great occasion, celebrated by all who were happy for us.

Things were going great. I had my lovely new home, and my lovely wife, and we were happy together.

I could always rely on my family when times got dangerously hard, especially when I had a stroke, and even more so when I needed a stem cell transplant—they all stepped up to the plate and tested themselves to be donors. Even my brother-in-law, who wasn't compatible, put himself on the register in the US. However, when my younger brother found out that he was 100 percent compatible and a full match, he automatically volunteered to be my donor. He said it would be an honour. This is true kinship, and anything I can do for him in the future, I will be right there, without a second's hesitation.

The three people that stood by me in my hour of need were my sister, Bola (who shocked me by coming all the way from the US to be there for me when I was to go into hospital), my brother Gbenga (who was my star donor), and my wife, Julie (who instigated the crowd funding and was by my side all the way).

My wife is incredible: She took in stride every piece of bad news that came along, and tried to find a solution to it; she stood by me when I needed her the most; and she took it upon herself to raise funds for my treatment. This all shows how warm, generous, and kind hearted she is—an absolute superstar!

Overall, I can say that I feel blessed with the family I have, as well as with the one I married into. They are all just great people.

Reflections

Now you know what drives me, and how I stay calm and focused. Is there something that has helped your wellness? Do you do something to help with your strength and stamina?

Insights from My Life

What can be said about what I have been through in my years on this planet, is that it has framed my outlook on life and how I approach everything I do, and the way I act around people.

Fortitude

When people say that I can't do something, I tend to react in the same way all the time. For example, when they said that I couldn't do my O-level selection or A-level selection, it really annoyed me, to the point where I desperately wanted to prove them wrong. If anyone tells you that you cannot do something, because they don't think you are smart enough, it is coming from either a place of jealousy or a place of superiority, and they are trying to make you look bad or stupid.

Try your best to prove them wrong, as you can become anything you want to be, if you are prepared to put in the hard work and do anything it takes to do so.

Have you ever heard people at work say, "Don't tell him too much?" Is it because they fear that you will take their job, or that someone might realise that they actually do nothing all day? I actually have always disagreed with this statement, because a good manager doesn't have to fear someone taking their job, as they might be promoted themselves. I think that teaching somebody all that there is, in order to do a job right, is a plus that comes with a lot of advantages:

1. You will have a reliable understudy.
2. You will know that the job will be done correctly.
3. You will be seen as a great coach, instructor, or mentor.

The Gift of Teaching

Something else I got from industry, and from working with so many companies over the years, is that I have a natural talent for teaching people things they need in order to do their jobs well; and they can go on to advance to higher roles, to reach their full potential. But this talent did not come easily to me; I had to work on it day by day, until I became a good teacher and an awesome coach—starting with taking time to study and understand the people whom I had to train, and adjust my sessions to suit.

In terms of my employment, I was lucky to have worked with some amazing and understanding managers in my time. Once I explained to them that I had sickle cell anaemia, and what that means, they were very understanding.

Due to the hectic lifestyle I used to live—travelling all over Europe and sometime the US—there was no real control I could put in place that would guarantee that I would not get a crisis, so I figured, if it happens, it happens. However, I tried not to get rattled, angry, or stressed, as I figured that would aggravate something. I took my tablets and painkillers as necessary, and just went with the flow. I found that this worked most of the time and. Luckily, the other times, I was on my way home anyway, so I went to hospital in Cambridge.

Learning to Breathe

The one thing that really helped me when I was away, was breathing techniques that I had learnt from martial arts. I learnt Tae Kwon Do at a dojo belonging to a friend, and he taught me how to defend myself and toughen up, without having to go through gradings. I would go into a meditative state and block everything out, breathing slowly and channelling my thoughts until I became totally relaxed and focused on one thing. This tended to reduce the pain I was in. Since I learnt this technique, I have always used it to calm myself down and reduce my pain.

Chapter 2

My Old Life

My Career Following University

My working life has always had its ups and downs, but life as a professional engineer was generally good. As long as I informed my employer up front of my condition with sickle cell anaemia, I was okay. Most of them were understanding. The main thing that I needed to work on was to not get stressed out in any way. This can trigger a crisis.

I figured that as long as I worked hard and stayed ahead of the game, nothing could hurt me. However, I learnt this and other lessons the hard way. In my first-ever manufacturing job, tragically, my boss broke his back while paragliding one weekend, and I had to fill in for him in many ways—doing the schedules, making sure products went out on time, etc. Then, to my surprise, someone walked into my office after a few months, telling me that he was the new production manager. This was a total surprise to me, as the managing director had not even told me that he was looking for one, let alone recruited someone.

By this time, I was working 12–15 hours a day; so I dialled it back to 8 hours a day, and let him get on with it. So, at some point, he had to ask me how to do certain parts of his job, and then he asked me about my future plans. I told him I was thinking of leaving, and within 2 weeks, I had found another job, and I resigned.

The biggest lesson I took home from that job was to never let anybody take advantage of you, and to only work agreed hours, even overtime hours. That way, you know where you stand in every way possible.

The next job, I thrived in, despite people wanting and trying desperately to get me out so that they could take over. I was there as a production planner, but I lasted four and a half years, and became a plant manager and deputy production manager. I outlasted most of the people that tried to get me out, and I fired a few of them. It was only because they shut down the plant that I left that job. Then I decided to do a complete U-turn and work as a JD Edwards functional consultant. In one go, I almost doubled my salary, and I changed my career.

I worked as a permanent employee for five years, until I convinced my last employer to make me redundant, and then I went solo. I have been working as an independent contractor for the last fifteen years, and I love the freedom it gives me. I have been lucky enough to work in different countries all over the world, including the USA, Japan, Sweden, France, Italy, Germany, Holland, and many other places.

However, the one important thing you need to do is to inform your manager or your recruiter that you have sickle cell anaemia. They are very understanding, and if you get sick or end up in hospital, they will provide coverage for you until you are fit enough to continue.

You don't want to be in a place that will always be challenging to you, or a place where you have to keep justifying your position. You want to be in a place where you can relax and grow.

A Personal Message to Any Workforce Leaders

Managers and team leaders need to understand that having sickle cell disease is not the fault of the individual. They did not choose to get this nasty disease; it is inherited. They were just unlucky, and the odds were against them.

Please be kind and understanding when they tell you that they have sickle cell disease. They didn't have to tell you something that personal.

The relationship will work both ways. If you give them the leeway they need, they will give back in the hard work and productivity they produce. Most sickle cell people are hardworking and only want to do the job they are paid to do. It is not their fault that they have these crises. They will give you 100% outside these times.

It is important that a person with sickle cell anaemia (or any serious disease) knows their limits, and the important question is about the problem of absence from work, as they might sometimes be hospitalised. However, an individual with sickle cell disease must understand their limitations before taking on particular types of employment. For example, if the job is suitable, absence from work is often no more frequent than it would be for any other member of the work force.

Heavy manual work, jobs that cannot be interrupted to take fluids, jobs that involve extreme changes of temperature or jobs involving lowered oxygen concentration are unsuitable for people with SCD.

Company Equality Policy Considerations

The equality policy should consider:

- Part-time hours or job sharing
- A well heated working environment
- Flexible working hours (working from home as necessary)
- Allowing employees to sit down (leg ulcers are a common symptom)
- Providing water and other fluids

- Allowing time off for hospital appointments, etc. (e.g., people may need dialysis 3 times a week)

Sickle cell is a condition that can easily be exacerbated by stress, temperature change, dehydration, exertion, and infection, so any policy should seek to reduce this and create a suitable working environment.

If your manager is unapproachable, it is important to follow through and see someone in the human resources department in your company. Talk to them so that it is on record, and they can put something in place to help your environment, or to help you get the time off you need to go to your doctor appointments.

How Medical Advice Has Changed Since the 70s

The advice that they gave patients in the 70s and 80s, differs so much from the advice that is given to patients nowadays.

Exercise:

For example, in the 70s and 80s, they told me that exercise was not advisable in any way or form, because it would bring on some sort of a crisis, which may put me in hospital or just bring on extreme pain. This I took on, word for word. I stayed away from exerting myself too much in any way. I even got myself a sick note, year after year, to avoid the school cross-country events, and to avoid physical education.

It wasn't until the late eighties, when my curiosity levels peaked in the line of rugby, that I started playing the game. I basically ignored the instructions I was given, and played half of two, half-hour sessions, to prevent exertion or a crisis. I have also played rugby with a mild crisis before. This was my way of doing things, but nowadays, it is recommended that you do physical exercise, but not too much as to exert yourself.

The advice is to do two and a half hours of exercise per week, but talk to your doctor about this before you start. I used to do more than that, but in the last 30 years, I have always trained hard.

Stress:

Stress is said to be hard to avoid, and it can trigger a crisis within the body; so try to take time out to relax, and try to find techniques that will help calm you down. I have always taken on serious challenges in the work place, and I have always found ways of coping, even if it was just to take five minutes out, every hour, to take a walk and calm myself down, before resuming the job at hand. I also found that deep relaxation techniques, such as meditation, are good for you, and re-energise your body to fight another day.

Some advice that is always given is to avoid any heavy lifting that will leave you breathless, which is only slightly true; but it is up to the individual that is doing the heavy lifting. I, myself, have done heavy lifting in certain jobs, but I have gone through some training to prevent being injured. I also do some heavy weight training exercises in my exercise regime, and have always done so for the last ten years, but I do not get any crises from that.

Flying:

Only travel using commercial airlines. This is good advice, but it is not the entire story. I have travelled in other types of aircraft, because I wanted to experience life. I have jumped out of a plane to do a parachute jump. Once, I also had to fly in a small propeller plane to cross the Maldives and get to another island. The point is, if it is a short flight, under an hour, it should be fine, because these flights normally don't go higher than 15,000 feet.

However, you will need to stick to certain advice like glue, because it can prevent you from getting sick. For example, don't go to high altitude places, like Denver (the mile-high city), as it can cause altitude sickness, which will trigger a crisis. Stay hydrated at all times, to prevent dehydration, and the eventual crisis. Stay warm in the cold, treat any infection straight away, etc.

Peak of Success

Some people would ask, "What would you know about success?" If they only knew what I've been through! I have been on the verge of losing it all and not being able to pay my bills—even driven to despair sometimes.

Five or six years ago, I was a very happy man indeed. I had it all, in abundance. I was on my way to saving money in the bank, making six figures a year, with a seriously thriving business, and I was a seriously happy and newly married man.

This was not easily done, as the taxman always found new ways of chasing me for money every time I had it. It wasn't fair, and it certainly wasn't fun at all. I was certainly at the peak of my career, where I was getting contracts easily, before I had finished one, so I had the next one lined up ready to go. No, I wasn't obsessed with work; but yes, people knew who I was in industry—they knew my reputation, and wanted to work with me.

On one hand, this was great, but on the other hand, I was hardly getting enough time off to be with my wife, except if I were to go on holiday, which we tried to do, once a year. But this life was certainly exhausting. I was doing things on autopilot, sometimes not even noticing which country I had crossed over to.

I was trying to find new ways of saving money and providing for my family, when it all went wrong.

It all went drastically wrong... I had a stroke in January 2015, and for the next seven to eight months, I was on rehabilitation.

Facing the Truth

It is a shock to me how many parents in this day and age are still in denial about their child having sickle cell anaemia. It is as if they are ashamed of their own child, or embarrassed that they could be responsible for inflicting such a painful disease on someone else, yet alone someone they created. Sickle cell is not a shameful disease; it is something that is inherited, and you can't do anything about that—certainly not in Africa. The only thing you could do is alter your children's genes medically, before birth, and to me, that is just wrong.

You should stand up and be counted. Otherwise, think of how the child is going to feel while growing up with the disease, and how they will feel when they get their first crisis. They need to be protected, yes; but they don't need to be sheltered from it.

I struggled as a child with sickle cell, because I was diagnosed around the same time that I was to supposed go away to school in the UK. I was soon the only black person at the school as well, let alone the only one with sickle cell. At that point, I didn't know what it was, and I didn't properly understand it. I just followed the instructions and advice that I was given by the school nurses. However, the more I grew up, the more I started taking control of my illness.

Also, the more I grew up, the more I decided what was right for me and what was wrong. I was still against cross-country runs because I didn't see the point in running 5k or 10k for no reason whatsoever. It wasn't until I left school that I found my love for rugby, and it wasn't until I hit the fifth form that I found my love for getting fit and keeping fit. I found my love for training in the school gym, and training with weights.

I started playing about with the dos and don'ts, and found the medium for myself personally. More people knew about my sickle cell anaemia when I got to university, but it didn't bother me. It was more of a relief than anything else.

Friends tried to understand and even to help, but I didn't care what other people thought. However, the one thing I did regret was not reconnecting with the sickle cell society for another twenty-five years. However, it is important that if there is anything you are struggling with, or any question you many have, that you just reach out to them. They are very nice, friendly, and extremely approachable.

I dealt with having sickle cell anaemia for forty-five years of my life, and it would have been even longer if it weren't for the fact that it tried to kill me with two strokes, and the fact that another one may have had a fatal result. I had to do something about it.

Reflections

From this chapter, you have learnt what it is to have sickle cell, how the blood flows and causes sickle cell crisis, what to look out for and avoid, how it is inherited, and that you must stand up and be counted. Do you or someone close to you have sickle cell? When did you find out, and how has it changed your life?

Part 2

Health Crisis and the End of My Old Life

Chapter 3

Managing Life's Curve Balls

The First Stroke

I had been working abroad for weeks, and I had just finished my contract. So, it was the first week that I had been a home for a while. We went to bed around 10 pm on Tuesday night, and I woke up around 7:30 am on Wednesday, the 21st of January, 2015, feeling quite peculiar. My wife had already gone to work.

I got up out of bed despite feeling peculiar, and headed to the bathroom to first brush my teeth. It was strange… I couldn't pick up or hold my toothbrush. All I felt was tingling in my hand, and my hand was positioned in a strange way, partially cupped with the fingers set apart from each other.

It took me what felt like a long time to brush my teeth, and then I jumped into the shower, only to find that this was a virtually impossible task, as I couldn't hold onto any of the cleaning implements. Once I eventually finished, I rang my wife to tell her what was happening, and she came right back home and took me to the doctors.

The doctor spoke to me for five minutes and then immediately sent me to hospital—she thought I might have had a stroke!

We headed to hospital, and the minute I said what had happened, I was whisked off to a bed in Accident and Emergency. I was approached by a nurse, who began to do some tests. Then I was sent for an x-ray and an MRI. I then saw a couple of stroke nurses, who just stood by my bed and asked a lot of questions. They tried to establish what had happened, and around what time it had happened. The MRI showed that it was a large TIA stroke. The time couldn't be established, so they assumed that it had happened during the night. (Because they weren't certain if it was within a six-hour window—in which case, they could reverse the stroke—I would have to go through the regular treatment.)

I was moved to a stroke ward on the other side of the hospital, and put through a stroke treatment, but what I really struggled with was meal times. This was extremely difficult as I had lost the use of my right hand, and I would have to teach myself to use it again, starting with some basic skills.

I was in hospital for a week, which was hard, as I was in a ward with very senior people who had had more serious strokes than I had. Also, I refused to leave before they sorted me out with proper physiotherapy outside the hospital, and some speech therapy, as I had severe slurring of my words during my stroke.

Once everything was arranged and I was fit enough to get up and about, I left the hospital.

The Rehab

Once I was out of hospital, the rehab really began. I had a stress ball that I constantly played with in my hand, consistently rolling it around in my hand and squeezing it. I also had a series of finger and wrist straightener's, which I squeezed every hour for six hours a day to strengthen them. On the fun side, my wife and I played a children's game, where you would have to pick up small plastic objects with a little hook. This helped with my dexterity.

My community physio person came around a few times to give me some extra exercises to do, which I dutifully did. A week after I was out of hospital, I had to go back every week to see the speech therapist. She went through some exercises with me every week: some tongue twisters and some readings. She stretched my vocabulary to the maximum and back again. My speech gradually started to improve with time, and got faster. I no longer sounded like I was a stroke victim.

Unfortunately, I woke up one morning with Bell's palsy, and my face drooped again. This was a setback I didn't need, but I continued with my rehab, and within a two-week period, the Bell's palsy went away. I carried on with my speech therapy and physio over the next few months, and I got stronger and stronger every day.

After about six months, it was time to get another job. I was approached by a company I used to work for, and they said that I could work from home 2 to 3 days a week, and all I had to do was assist with their implementation of SAP. This was perfect as it wasn't too far to get to work, and I could work at my own pace. It was the perfect job at the time.

However, when I started working, I realised that there was something missing. I had lost parts of my memory that had to do with the things I used to know instantly and was able to execute without any problems. I feared that my knowledge of configuring a system like JD Edwards ERP systems was lost. I quickly made an appointment with my therapist to discuss this, and to find out whether there was anything I could do to get it back. She recommended that I see a hypnotherapist, and referred me to one.

At this point, I was so desperate to gain every ounce of memory back, and I was willing to try anything. I went to see this nice woman several times, and each time I did, she put me into a deep meditative state, where I was extremely calm and relaxed. She talked to me calmly, and with each session, I started to gain parts of my memory back. All I had to do then was to join the dots, and let the brain find and develop new pathways to access the memories.

With that done, I felt close to being whole again. I was able to write, type, and use my right hand as well as I used to, and my speech was as good as it was ever going to be. I felt good—almost whole again.

The only thing stopping me from returning to my previous life was the Friday blood transfusions.

The Diagnosis

A couple of months after the stroke, I was called to the hospital in Cambridge to see my doctor. He said they suspected that the stroke was caused by my sickle cell anaemia! Did I mention that I had sickle cell anaemia? So that they could prevent it from happening again, their recommendation was to try and reduce the amount of sickle blood in my body, from around 60–70%, down to under 30%, and eventually 20%.

They wanted to start as soon as possible. This meant that every Friday, for the foreseeable future, would be spent at hospital, with them withdrawing two units of blood and then giving me back another two units of blood. The first two or three were very painful, before I got used to them. After about a year of these transfusions, my veins were shot to pieces, and I had to have a "pick line" fitted and attached to my jugular vein.

This made access easier for the nurses when they wanted to give me blood. The only problem was that the venesection still needed to be done in my arms, to withdraw the two units of blood to be exchanged. This went on for a few more months, until I started questioning the doctors as to other treatments out there.

I was told of a treatment that was at the trial stage in the US, called Stem Cell Transplant, for sickle cell patients, and Kings College Hospital in London was trying to get it done here. I convinced my doctor to arrange for a referral to the doctor at Kings College Hospital. Her name was Dr. Victoria Potter, and the procedure in question was invented by a Dr. J. Tisdale.

We went to see her, and she explained the procedure and the expected outcome with us. She said she could arrange for me to have it done in the US. I left the hospital with some newfound hope.

I spent the next few months researching this procedure and contacting some private hospitals in London to see if they would carry out the procedure, and how much it would cost. The average cost that was thrown at us was £120,000! That was a shock and an unreachable target. Then a doctor said to ask my own doctor, as she would probably be able to do it much cheaper. So, that is just what I did. I rang her up and asked her out right. She said she would think about it, and come up with a figure in three days.

A few days later, she came back to me with £70,000. It seemed like an unreachable task, but my lovely tenacious wife got right to it. She set up a crowdfunding page, and started asking people she/we knew to donate. It went out to all my friends (old and new), colleagues, her workmates, and anybody else we knew. It was tough, but she rallied on, not too dissuaded to give up.

Eventually, we had raised up to £55,000, which was enough to get the hospital to start the procedure. Meanwhile, they tested everyone in my family for potential donors, and my brother turned out to be a 100% full sibling match—the best there could be.

The Second Stroke

My second stroke was uneventful, really. I was out with some friends, whom I hadn't seen for a long time due to other commitments and some living across the world, and my wife. We were sitting in a pub, relaxing and chatting away. Then, suddenly, I felt a little odd, and I went cold and then hot again.

I did nothing about it at first, and then my wife asked me if there was something wrong, as she had noticed that I was preoccupied and fidgeting a lot. I told her that nothing was wrong, but then I thought about it some more: "I think I have had another stroke!" Then we decided to call it a night as it was about 11 o'clock in the evening.

Rather than going to hospital, we went home, and I slept on it. I woke in the morning to find that the section below my left elbow, to above my left hand, was tingling and numb, and felt a little strange.

I decided to go to hospital, and I was seen fairly quickly at first, but then I spent a couple of hours in A&E, waiting to see a doctor, as they argued between each other on whose care I should go under— haematology or the stroke unit. Due to the position in which I had had the stroke, there was nothing they could really do physically with the arm. However, they made a decision to double up on the blood transfusions I have. Also, I was to receive six units of blood over the three days I was to be in hospital, to force my sickle cell percentage down to 23%, starting as soon as they could get the blood. The blood had to come from Bristol, as there was only one donor in the entire country with matching blood.

I did a lot of tests, received my blood transfusions, and took in a lot of fluid. My doctor became very worried at this stage, because the risk of another stroke went up again, and the next one could be fatal or could result in me becoming disabled; so he informed Dr. Potter at

Kings College Hospital in London. This was the reason to expedite things and bring forward the test that had to be done.

The only set back was that another blood test showed the fact that I had latent TB. This would have to be treated before the transplant could go ahead. This is due to the fact that when my immune system gets reduced to zero, the TB may come alive, and I would not have the means to fight it. This may result in death. It was hard to swallow this piece of news, but I had to, and I started the three months' treatment of TB antibiotics to clear it. After it was over, I got the all clear for latent TB, and I was given a date to start the treatment, which was February 27th, 2017.

Reflections

You have discovered about my strokes, how they happened, what I did to recover from them, and the gruelling rehab I had to undertake. Go to the next chapter to find out about the repercussions of having these strokes, and what happened next.

How would you feel if you or someone close to you had a stroke? Are you the kind of person to push your rehab, or would you let someone else take the lead?

Chapter 4

The Repercussions

My Blood Transfusions

Once the first stroke was over, and I was in rehab mode, I was summoned to discuss the next actions that the hospital needed to take for my health. They discussed having blood transfusions, starting with two units of blood every week. Starting that week, on Friday morning, I was to report to the Haematology Day Unit, at 9 am.

Once I arrived, they talked me through the procedure and asked me to sit on a bed. They would start with a venesection (the removal of two units of blood). The nurse raised the bed up and put a large needle in my arm. She taped it up, and then she let gravity do its own thing.

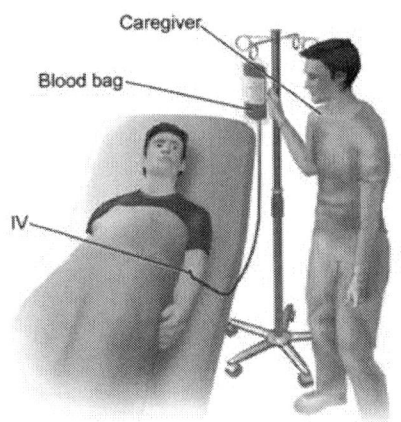

Blood Transfusion

The blood came rushing out of my arm, filling the bag up quickly. She then changed the bag to fill up the next bag. Still, blood rushed out of my arm, and still rather quickly, it filled up the second bag.

The nurse then placed some pressure on my arm, removed the needle, and stemmed the blood. Once it was taped up, the next thing to do was to hook me up with the first unit of blood. It takes approximately 90 minutes per unit of blood to be intravenously given. In the meantime, I just have to lie down and relax, or do a little bit of work while I wait for the first and second units of blood to go through. The point of this was to replace my damaged sickle shaped blood cells with healthy blood cells. However, it may take longer than the allotted time, because the day unit may be very busy.

This went on every week for fourteen months, non-stop, including the Christmas holidays. It was so frequent that my veins on both arms blew and were of no use for six to twelve months. They then had to put a heavy-duty pick line into my chest, for easy access to my blood. I chose not to have local anaesthetic during the procedure, which I regretted, as it was so painful. Luckily, it only took 30 minutes.

I would have to say though, that having the blood transfusions every Friday almost destroyed my career. I could no longer get a contract outside the UK, and within the UK, nobody wanted to hire a contractor, on a JDE project, on a part-time basis or for four days a week.

Then, suddenly, a miracle happened (or a postulate). I had a call from a company I used to work with, offering me a job for as long as I would like it, and I could work a couple of days a week at home. I chose Fridays to do work at home, but instead of being at home, I chose to work at the hospital and do the transfusion at the same time. This was some clever lateral thinking on my behalf (i.e. the ability to utilise all resources one has at one's disposal).

Keeping a Sense of Normality

It was important to me to try and get back to some form of normal life. So, getting back to work was a big thing for me. Things aren't given to you; you need to work for yourself, and good things come to you when you work for yourself.

While I was going through the transfusions, I couldn't help thinking that there must be an alternative to this out there. I tried to look things up on the internet and in medical papers, and eventually I had to ask my doctors to find out some other treatments.

On another point, I wanted to start building a passive income stream for my family and my retirement, so that I wouldn't have to rely on the pittance that the government might give me on retiring. So, I started looking at the business of affiliate marketing, with my wife. I dabbled at first, to understand everything about the business and the industry.

I set up a business and began studying again, investing a huge amount of money in my education. I looked at things in detail, dissected things in detail, and broke things down to minute degrees. Then I started building things back up slowly, to the point where my wife and I got going. We started making inroads in affiliate business. However, something didn't feel right, so we pulled the plug on the business in order to analyse things in more detail.

We decided to put everything on hold for a while, when we discovered something new. We explored things and realised that we were being attracted by *the new shiny object* syndrome. Then we created our first training program, which in time, we fine-tuned as we learnt more.

We then decided to go back to affiliate marketing, very slowly, with small advertising budgets, and advertise our own training. We achieved more success with this, and we made a few realisations about our business as well.

My consultancy business, on the other hand, took such a hit with my illness, and I almost filed for liquidation. I was pulled out of it, with difficulty and on the brink, and I did all I could to pay the HMRC and start operating again.

I really struggled to get out of the situation my company was in, as I wasn't allowed to work for the first six months out of hospital with the first stroke. I concentrated on getting fit, and on my rehabilitation. I went on walks and went to the gym, and I did therapy to get my head right.

The Fight for My Life

Very soon after Dr. Potter explained the protocol for the stem cell transplant, she applied for the funding to do the operation. This was rejected straight away, on the grounds that the NHS (National Health Service) considered the procedure too dangerous and not worth the risk.

This wasn't acceptable. We immediately put in another application for the funds, backing it up by having several doctors state how much I needed this stem cell transplant. The case was so strong, and it was explained that this was an application for a single person, not an application for all. It was also explained that the protocol for a fully matched sibling donor was ninety-four percent successful in the US, and very little could go wrong.

This application was also rejected for the same reasons, including parts of the NHS panel not believing in American medicine, and others not believing that the protocol could work. Most of the panel were not doctors, and basically, the decision they made was not based on looking at the data presented in front of them—and it was a little bit racist. The whole report that came back was very negative.

It was very evident that the reasons they gave for their rejection were not based on the evidence put in front of them. They gave reasons such as, "It is too risky," and "We don't recognise American medicines," and "We need to conduct our own research and trials first." These were the funniest of reasons, as they wouldn't even pay for a hospital to carry out a trial, or for the frequently used medicines from America (but in this case, it was for sickle cell), and they have been left behind by a number of countries in regard to treatments, like US, France, and even India. They should be ashamed of themselves.

I was so incensed about it all, I even agreed to do a series of interviews with the press.

Medical Costs – The Sky Was the Limit!

Because of this, we appealed and sent in further proof, and they still rejected our application. So, we started finding out how much it would cost to have the protocol done privately. We contacted some of the private hospitals, and visited them, including the London Clinic. After talking to them, we realised that the cost of this treatment was very, very expensive—in the region of £120,000.

One of the doctors we spoke to suggested going back to our doctor and asking her what it would cost for her to do the protocol herself, as most of the private doctors in these hospitals are also NHS doctors.

So, we asked Dr. Potter, and she said to give her a couple of days to come up with the cost. She came back, three days later, with a breakdown of the costs, totalling £70,000. We agreed to pay the price, and my wife almost immediately went to work and set up a crowdfunding page. She sent it to everybody she knew, including my friends, and I decided to send it to my university friends, as well as some of my work colleagues.

We did everything we could to make money, including organising charity dinner dances, running high quality raffles, and anything else we could think of at the time. Some friends really stepped up to help us organise things, and others did their own thing to raise money for me. It was really humbling, and I was extremely grateful for their help.

With the help of all our savings and friends and family, we saved £55,000 for the transplant, which was enough to get the process started, and we paid it to the hospital.

Channel 4 News to the Rescue

During my battle with the National Health Service, my wife tried to get coverage of the story with the local media, but they were not interested. At the same time, I had reconnected with the Sickle Cell Society. They invited me to their office in London, as they were doing an interview with Channel 4 health correspondent, Victoria McDonald. I agreed to go, and when I got there, they interviewed the chairman on his views on stem cell transplants for sickle cell. They took me to a coffee shop and asked me to tell them my story, and then they asked me how I felt about the NHS rejecting the funding application.

I was clear and direct in my answers, and told them exactly what I thought about NHS bureaucracy in wasting money on pointless treatments, and propping up sick people rather than addressing real illnesses with proper cures. I also told them that they have already spent twice the amount to cure me by just propping me up, with little quality of life, and living with a potential death sentence.

Victoria agreed with Toby (the story finder) to run with my story, and they asked if they could cover one of my weekly transplants. I said they could, but they would have to get permission from the hospital to film there. They got the permission within forty-eight hours and were there on the Friday morning to film everything, and they asked me a few more questions. The first media piece was done and out on air the following week, which to me was amazing.

They then asked me if it was okay if they filmed my stem cell transplant for sickle cell. They asked me to think about it, because it would be while I was very vulnerable. I got back to them the following week, after talking it through with my wife, and said it would be fine.

They then took to interviewing my doctor and getting permission to film at Kings College Hospital in London. Victoria and Toby filmed my arrival to hospital, and then came back to film the transplant procedure. Then they filmed me again when I got home, after the whole thing was over.

They put it all together, and it came out as the second extended piece of Channel 4 News. The whole compilation was an absolute genius piece of journalism. It made the front-line staff of the NHS look absolutely professional—but it made the back-office management look very stupid indeed to have denied this procedure to anybody who needed it.

The coverage of the whole story was done in a very professional manner. Ever since then I have had numerous comments by strangers on the street and by friends of friends, about how they never realised the existence of sickle cell anaemia, or that it could have such an effect on people's lives. Some even went on to comment on the shame of the NHS, and their shock at finding that they would stop looking for a cure for people in this country, and waste money on trivial matters that come up.

This was what we set out to achieve from these interviews, and we succeeded with that and more.

Reflections

By now you should have a pretty good idea about what I went through, and that I don't give up easily. Actually, I never give up, ever. If I believe that I have a right to live, or anyone else, I would fight tooth and nail for them. If you or a loved one were in my situation, what would you advise them to do?

Chapter 5

My Transplant

Before the Treatment

Once it was agreed that I was going to go through with this protocol, it was also agreed that Dr. Potter would follow this protocol at Kings College Hospital. Five months before the protocol, I was told to get physically fit, and to come to hospital with a positive mind set.

Time to Get in Shape

I started by going to the gym four days a week, and I was working with a trainer for the first time. I got my friend, Joe Ison, to train me. Joe is one of those trainers that actually bothers to get to know their clients, their goals, their strengths and weaknesses, and their ambitions. He creates training programs to fit the individual, rather than the other way around.

He worked me hard. He increased my stamina and endurance. I increased my strength and improved my mental health. My fitness levels went up with every exercise I did. Whether it was cycling, rowing, running, or boxing, or doing squats, Romanian dead lifts, bench presses, shoulder presses, chest flies, triceps extensions, etc., everything was handled, and all obstacles were faced head on.

Mind...Yes It Does Matter

The next thing to tackle was my mindset. To do this, I began by reading and understanding everything I could get my hands on about the stem cell transplants and how they work, and what to expect to go through. I went to each part of the protocol individually, and looked at all the side effects at each stage, and wrote everything down until it was drummed into me. I did everything I could to understand everything, and I was happy about it. The next thing to do was to get some inner peace and be happy with myself, and with everything.

I went out with my wife several times for dinner. We had several business meetings, and I put her at ease about going through the whole protocol, as she would be on the outside of this whole process, like a spectator. I also spoke to a few select friends, and put my life in order with my solicitor.

I was now set to go into hospital. I was ready, my mind was clear, and I was positive that everything was going to go well. If I had any hitches, I knew what to do to overcome them. All my papers were in order, and I was fitter than I had been for fifteen years or so.

The next stop: hospital!

The Day of the Transplant

I had a phone call telling me that I had to come into hospital a week earlier for some tests and a little top-up of blood, so I agreed.

When I got there, I settled into my room, in a private ward, and they took some blood for tests, and I was told to get a good night's rest. The next day, I was sent down to the exchange unit for a six-unit blood exchange, which would take 5 hours to do. The neat trick is that they withdraw blood out of one arm, and put blood back in through the other arm. The only thing I could do was just lie there and relax.

The Next Few Days

The next day, I was to go down to the theatre to have a Hickman line fitted, as they refused to use my pick line. It hurt for three or four days, but that was it. As I was lying there in bed, I had a visit from a lady who said she was a hospital psychologist. She then came right out and asked me, "Are you depressed?" I looked at her and said, "Sorry?" She said, "A lot of people get depressed in hospital, so we just want to check that you are not one of them." I told her that I had nothing to be depressed about, and that I was being cured of my illness, so I was in a good place. She said she would come back in seven days. Meanwhile, I was moved to the transplant ward.

The next day, Monday, I started the protocol. I received my first dosage of Campath (a low dosage of the immunosuppressant), along with Sirolimus (organ transplant rejection drugs) and other drugs. I felt nothing at the time— no side effects or anything. Then the next thing I knew, I was being woken up by a nurse around midnight. She took my temperature and said that it was a little high, and that she would notify the doctor of this.

The next day was the same: I took the drugs, got a high temperature in the night, and so forth. This went on for five days, with my temperature going up to 41, 42, 40, and 43, before easing back down to normal. Every day, I walked around my room excessively, about 30–40 times, to relieve boredom.

On the sixth day, I was picked up by ambulance and transported to Guys Hospital for the radiotherapy treatment. This was the bit I feared the most, as I was basically put in the position of a spit roast, and radiated all over. Afterwards, you begin to shiver, and I was so cold that they had to put a blanket over me. Then they discovered that no ambulance had come to pick me up, so they had to call my ward at Kings College Hospital and arrange with them to get an ambulance to pick me up.

When I got back, I went straight to bed and went to sleep, ignoring all my visitors. The next day was to be a rest day, with no treatments whatsoever—just a chance for me to sleep, relax, and chill out.

On Wednesday, March 15th, I was prepared to receive the stem cells from my donor, my brother. I knew how hard it had been for him, so I waited patiently upstairs. I waited over half the day, and then the nurse walked into the room and asked if I was ready. I smiled and said, "Yes." This was to be the beginning of my new life. This was to be day one. The stem cells were given to me intravenously. It took just 15 minutes to give this to me, and then it was all over. I couldn't believe it! Such an anti-climax; however, I was so elated!

Now for the hardest part: sitting around for twenty-one days whilst waiting for my immune system to kick back in, and for the levels to start going up.

The greatest hero that I have ever known was the one who saved my life–My Brother!!!

Reflections

Whoa, that is some serious stuff, you are thinking. But remember this: If I didn't have this, I could have another stroke that could potentially disable or kill me. If you were in the same situation, what would you do? So, read on to see what happened when I went through it.

Chapter 6

Sometimes Things Have to Go Wrong
in Order to Go Right

I often say that a strong mindset was what brought me through my long stay in hospital, but that was not all. I had to deal with things on a day-by-day basis, and my mind was up and down like a bouncing ball.

At first, when I went into hospital, I was upbeat. I was positive that I was doing the right thing, and that everything would turn out well. I mean, thirty days in hospital couldn't be that bad, right? After all, I had books to read, videos to watch, and enough work to do for thirty days and beyond.

Then came day number 2. I had to have another line placed into my chest. A Hickman line was put in for the transplant and the blood exchange of 6 units. This was done under a local anaesthetic; but an hour afterwards, when it started to wear off, the pain was so bad, and I began to doubt whether this was a good idea. I mean, if that part was hurting that much, what would the rest of it be like?

But then I shook it out of my head, thinking about the greater good. I had to talk to myself to concentrate on the end game. It was a small price to pay for the greater good.

I Really Thought I Was Going to Die

Then came my next challenge, on day three of the treatment. I received the third increase of the Campath dosage, and it wasn't until later that evening that my temperature started to rise. I felt really hot as the nurse came in to take my temperature. It was 42.5 degrees Celsius. That scared me a little. I had never felt like that before. My thoughts were all over the place. This couldn't be logical. *Am I dying?* I thought to myself, as I slowly nodded off to sleep.

The following morning, I was up and raring to go again, feeling like I could conquer the world. Then, days later, after my radiation session, I started shaking as I was cold, and I started to wonder if it was all worth it. I dug deep into my thoughts and remembered that I had known what I was going to go through, and what side effects could occur. Then I told myself: "Snap out of it. Get a grip. This is happening for one reason: to prevent yourself from having another stroke, and to rid yourself of the disease that has been holding you back for years."

I prayed to God that night, and the next morning, my mindset kicked back into the positive. I had the day off from any treatment, and just chilled out by watching videos, sleeping, and doing nothing.

The following day was what it was all about: the transplant day. I was up and ready to go, feeling so happy and looking forward to it. However, I sat around most of the day, until 5 pm, when they came in to prep me. Then, the nurses came with a small bottle and attached it to the line, and off we went. In 15 minutes, it was all over. What they took from my brother, for over six hours, they put into my arm in 15 minutes—that was insane. Then comes the waiting game.

I must now wait for my immune system to wake up, now that I have new stem cells starting to produce blood in my body. This is where I had to be strong, and my mindset took over to perform my thinking for me. I planned everything out on the board on the wall, and my nurses recorded my blood results on a daily basis so that I could monitor how my body was behaving with the new system. My neutropenes, haemoglobin, and a number of other results were all monitored, and I had something to aim for.

While this was all going on, I had plenty of time to work on my businesses, even though I was not allowed to work for at least six to eight months.

Emotions of the Mind

The entire journey had been an emotional roller coaster. I remember the first night that I had spent in hospital, before the treatments started, and when my brother and my wife had gone home. I was lying down on the bed in my room, alone, staring at the ceiling. I was exhausted, and I thought to myself, "Finally! This was what all the drama was for. All those arguments with the NHS, all the fund raising—everything has come to this."

I suddenly shivered. Things have to go right. Things must go to plan. I suddenly felt scared and worried. Then I put it out of my head.

I fell asleep, and that night was the first night's deep sleep I had had in the last two months. I woke up upbeat and ready to face anything.

During the first week that I was in hospital, I was really pushed to the limits. The minor operation to get the Hickman line into my chest was so painful, and it felt so uncomfortable for the first couple of days—I almost cried several times over.

Then, the Campath treatment was so strange. It felt okay at the beginning and during the day, but in the evening, and late at night, I would feel so hot and uncomfortable, and I would toss and turn most of the night.

It was hard to keep control all the time. However, I would constantly find myself talking to myself to get a grip. I would always tell myself: "Focus on the end game. You are stronger than this, and it is for the greater good." I would also remind myself of the benefit of getting through it all and not having sickle cell anaemia any more.

All these positives got me through the dark days, and my wife and family distracted me enough to minimise the time that I was left alone to think.

When the conditioning and the treatment was over, that was when I was glad that my mindset training and logical mind could take over, and I started monitoring my statistics on a spreadsheet (what my blood results were every day). I monitored everything so closely that I knew which days were good and which days were bad, before the doctors came in to see me. Every good day cheered me up so much that I would be on a high for that day. This went on until day 21, when the doctors came in and said that I was doing so well that I could go home. I was elated but said no, because nothing was arranged with my wife, as she was staying at her sister's, which was closer to the hospital but nowhere near our home. We spent that day arranging things so that I could go home the day after.

It just shows that having a positive mindset, faith, and a lot of determination can help with anything.

The Recovery Period

Dear friend, bid farewell to your bad health, and get ready to greet happiness and wellness!

I spent three weeks waiting around in the hospital, walking around the wards and waiting for my neutrophils to go up. The first few days, I would walk around the small room, counting my steps. It wasn't easy, as I could probably walk around the entire room in less than forty steps, but I would count up to five or even ten thousand steps.

The next stage was to venture out of my room and walk around the ward. This was fairly easy as it was only two long corridors, with side rooms off the corridors, and one recess room at one end of the corridors, linking the two together, and the exit on the other end.

After ten days, and after I had gained enough strength and boredom, I decided to venture out of the ward to walk up and down the corridors of the first and second floors of the hospital. I was so glad to have visitors throughout my stay in hospital, including my sister, who flew over from Connecticut, USA. My wife was by my side all the time; and my brother came to see me, even though he was having pain due to the drugs he had to take before getting his stem cells taken. These three people were regular visitors every day of the week, for most of the time. Then, when it was over, my sister went home.

I gained a new appreciation for anyone having to go through any cancer treatment, leukaemia treatment, or any blood related illness, as it is no fun at all. The treatments are severe and invasive, and some of the drugs and radiation are very painful indeed. I was lucky not to have many side effects at all, but I hear they can be brutal.

Is the NHS Missing the Bigger Picture? Quite Possibly!

On top of that, I proved something to the NHS. This is not a treatment of fantasies, and it is not something that was thought of on a whim. Stem cell transplants for sickle cell, with a fully matched sibling donor, really do work as they say it would. There is a success rate of over ninety-four percent. So, you would be stupid not to do it. You would be even more stupid not to fund something like this, which could save thousands of lives and save the NHS thousands of pounds every year, rather than just propping everyone up with transfusions every week.

Basically, it costs over £100,000 per year for a person to be propped up, with no fix, and having just two units a week. The blood alone is £400 per unit, which will cost £41,600, and hiring a bed at a conservative price of £250 will cost £13,000, plus x-rays, MRIs, needles, venesection kits, and the possibility of hospitalisation for one or two weeks—all giving a total greater than £100,000 over a twelve-month period.

It is ridiculous that the NHS and NICE are reluctant to look at and revise their protocols for the treatment of sickle cell disease and the like. It seems even more illogical, considering that synthetic stem cell transplants are now coming into play, as well as gene therapy. It is all happening so quickly in countries like the USA, Mexico, Italy, and France; and yet the UK seems blinkered. They are denying that it is happening, except when it suits them, as when someone really needs this treatment, the NHS Doctors arrange for them to be treated in the United States.

Time to Go Home

After fifteen days, my blood levels had gone up to an acceptable level, so they said I could go home. At this point, I said no. I had no keys to the house, I had no transport, and more importantly, my wife didn't know, as she was staying at her sister's. I called her, and we arranged for her to come and see me early in the morning. Then we arranged for the hospital to sort out transport and my discharge papers. This all took until four o'clock in the afternoon, and then I went home through London rush hour.

After I got home, and settled, I had to go back to hospital a week later, and then every two weeks, and then once a month. After 12–15 months, they cut the visiting time to every three months for the outpatient appointments. This was a good sign that all was going to plan. Then they started looking at cutting back on the anti-rejection drug, Sirolimus.

A week after I got home, my personal trainer, Joe, came to visit me, and he gave me a training session, as well as tips on gentle exercises I could do at home.

I also began to understand a lot more about life, and I was beginning to understand that I needed to change my life, now that I had been given a new one. I needed to change things around, and rather than running around the world chasing clients, I needed clients to come to me instead, and I needed to be selective about whom I work with.

Reflections

I can't believe that I survived all that! Wow, what a ride—the ups and downs, the fevers, the fun we had raising money, the exercises, and the mental challenges that I went through—all for survival!

How do you think you would cope in that situation? Would you do things differently?

Read on to find out what motivated me.

Part 3

Getting a Second Chance at Life

Chapter 7

Life After the Transplant

Support

My life after the transplant completely changed. First of all, financially, I was severely handicapped. If it weren't for some people (who I will mention in the next session), I would have been on the streets within a few months.

I had been seen by several support groups, and they went through my finances in detail. They all asked the question, "Surely, there must be something you could claim from the government for support?" They all looked it up, helped me fill out some forms, and were quite frankly surprised about the lack of help that exists for someone within their own company, or for someone who is self-employed, who get sick or hospitalised. The only thing I could have claimed was the incapacity allowance—and that only paid £50 per month, which was an insult to me. Then they all tried to refer me to the MacMillan Cancer Support charity, and although they were very sympathetic, they could not help, as I did not have cancer.

I could not believe it. I had dutifully paid my taxes and my National Insurance for twenty years, and everything was up to date, but when I needed help, there was none available. I began to ask the question: Why? What is the point of paying these things when you get nothing back when you need it the most?

Writing to my MP was pointless. I had tried to write to her before the transplant, and I found that she was absolutely useless. I got more action and answers from Amber Rudd, who was the MP of my father-in-law. I got very frustrated and eventually gave up.

For almost eight months, I could not and was not allowed to work, by the instruction of doctors. I had emptied my bank account, and had even emptied my business account in the first three months, just trying to survive. It was very frustrating indeed.

Luckily for me, I had a very good support network of friends, family, and my dear wife. If it weren't for them and my wife, I think I would have gone mad, been homeless, and in despair. Things just didn't look good at all.

The fact is that you need to be prepared to do anything it takes to survive. I started looking at what transferable skills I had, and what I could do online. This included getting paid for filling in questionnaires, answering people's questions about business issues, and getting paid to do some contract work remotely. All of this, I could do in my own time, as long as I hit realistic deadlines, giving me time to relax and even catch a few naps when I got tired. This was a way to survive while I was not allowed to officially work or even search for work.

In terms of things to do, I had a surprise the second week I was home, from my trainer, who came to my home and gave me some exercises I could do at home, to build my strength back up and to keep myself motivated. I found this very helpful indeed, because it got me through some dull moments; and I found my strength getting better day by day with that, and by going on walks as far as I could go.

Family

Family is a funny thing. Relationships and interactions can change day to day, but when things happen, they all come together.

I was shocked and happy to see my sister when she turned up unannounced at the hospital on my second or third day there. She instantly got to work doing what she does best. She asked the doctors a lot of questions about the transplant, keeping them on their toes. She also had a go at one or two nurses for their lack of cleanliness and just down right laziness. It provided me with great entertainment, and admiration to see someone care so much.

My younger brother, Gbenga, on the other hand, is like me in a lot of ways. He is very laid back but cares a lot. He would do anything for anyone he likes. He was my donor and my saviour. He would come in to visit me every day, and just sit around chatting and cheering me up. However, if he sees something wrong, he will stand up and challenge it. He is very smart and wise, and not to be underestimated. It is very comforting to know that he always has my back, and I will always have his.

The person that was most scared about all of the procedure was my mother. She called me every day to check on me, and wanted to know whether I was all right. Sometimes she would call three times in a day, just because she was worried. I know she would have been there if she could, but she was stuck in Nigeria. My youngest brother was also stuck in Nigeria and could not be there.

I had the support of my other sister and brother from afar, and it was comforting to know that they all rallied together to support me.

I also got a lot of support from my wife's sister and her father, but most of all from my wife. She was by my side from morning to night, almost every day that I was in hospital.

I can't tell you how stressful it must be to see your loved one go through a procedure that might, at worst, potentially kill them, but at best could save their life. So, I had to do everything I could to stay alive, and fight every obstacle that came up. Like I have always said, I am the lucky one.

However, you don't really appreciate things until you go through something like this, and come out the other side with a newfound appreciation for even the tiniest of things. Then you find that most people just get on with their lives and eventually ignore you. This was with the exception of my wife, my mother, and my brother, who still worry about me and constantly check up on me.

Motivation and Mindset

The most powerful thing to gain from all of this is to get a positive mindset and masses of motivation to get through anything, and to bulldoze through any obstacle that is put in your way.

Have a solid mindset that you can overcome any challenge or problem that is put in your way, and come up with unique ways of dealing with your issues. It motivates you to push past barriers and come up with unique ways of coming up with solutions for any issue.

As I have mentioned earlier, before I had to go into hospital, I had to get my mindset correct. This meant that I had to go in with a positive and determined mindset. To do this, I needed to study how minds work, and the types of mindsets you can have. After choosing the right one, I then studied how it could be developed. I found that a growth mindset could be enhanced and grown exponentially. The only thing stopping its growth is the limits you set on it.

I learned that you need to get out of your comfort zone to grow, and once you get out of that comfort zone, and push yourself past the fear that comes from that action, then you end up in the learning zone.

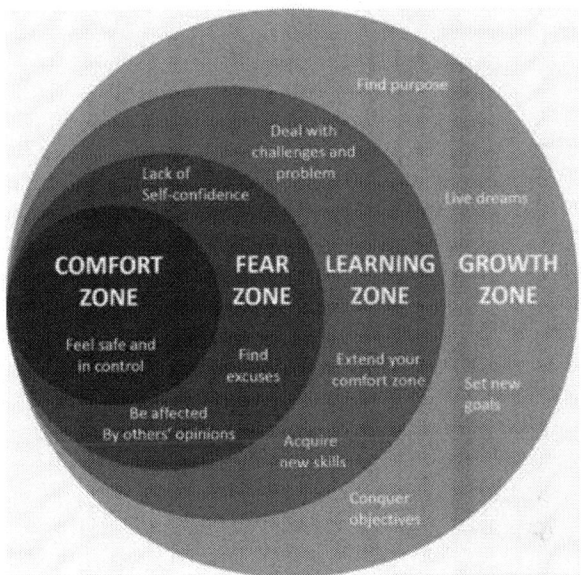

At this point, I learnt everything I could about my procedure, the side effects, the low points and the high points, and its success rate. Armed with all this knowledge, I grew more confident, happy, and ready to conquer all.

In fact, because I was so set on being able to cope with anything that could come along during the 21 days I was going to be in hospital, everyone commented on how well I was coping. The fact is, I knew when things would happen, and when things could go wrong, and I would do everything I could to avoid the lulls, even when the psychologist kept coming in every 8 days to ask if I was depressed yet. She was even surprised when I kept saying no. There was nothing that would take me by surprise, except for the speed of my recovery.

I have learnt how to put the same logic into my business, and to teach others how to do the same. With this as a part of their armour, there is nothing they can't overcome.

Back to Business

When I got out of hospital, I thought about things seriously, and realised that I had to find a new way of doing business. Although I had a lucrative business before I became ill, things had changed. I was no longer prepared to run halfway around the world chasing after clients who don't appreciate me, and who complain a lot of the time. Don't get me wrong; they are not all like that. Some are great to work with, and for. But to be honest with you, I have to find a better way. My wife and I had been thinking about it for a while, but now it is time to take action. Learning all we could about starting an online business, we got to work.

I thought about all the things I know, and how I could apply them, and it came to me like a bolt of lightning: I was going to be a coach on how to get your powerful "why," and how to create a positive mindset for growth and success. This would be taught to a targeted audience of new business owners, entrepreneurs, and people needing personal development.

You may ask me why I chose those two topics to coach; and the answer would be based on my life experiences. As I mentioned, when I came out of hospital, I was a changed man. No longer was I willing to chase clients across the world to solve their problems. Working with my wife, we decided that I need people to come to me, and then I could help them. I set up another business, and my "why" was to help and develop people who were wanting to set up a business for themselves, to grow and understand what would make them successful when things get hard. I also have a vision to build a hospital or a foundation to help treat people with blood diseases, whether it be sickle cell, thalassaemia, leukaemia, or blood cancer, to list a few.

My mindset, however, was developed, as explained in the previous section. The fact is, once you go through that kind of transformation in your mind, it is hard to forget it all; it stays with you for a long time, and it becomes part of you. I will always have a positive mindset and a growth mindset. I am always open to learning more and more things, and to grow further to success.

My business is starting to pick up, and it is gaining some momentum with some organising and advertising.

Reflections

Throughout all of this, I got some truths. Never rely on your own MP to help. The bottom line is that only you or your family can help you get things done. Never underestimate the power of your spouse. Also, you need to find ways of building your wealth without giving away your time for nothing. I love helping people, and with a powerful mindset, you can achieve anything. Do you have someone you can rely on? If you need help with your mindset, contact me at www.firstandonlynow.com.

Read on to find out more about the"other."

Part 4

Spirituality and Faith

Chapter 8

My Beliefs

When someone says that they do not believe in anything, I almost feel sorry for them.

I mean, there must be something in life that you believe in, surely. Whether it is yourself, your capabilities, your family—there must be something. If you say that there is nothing you believe in, surely you are on the road to nowhere. You are aiming at nothing, and you have no one to back you up at any stage of your life.

I don't care if you say to me, "I believe in aliens and extraterrestrial life." That is fine. If it works for you, and you are not joking, I can live with it. But believing in absolutely nothing, is a sure-fire way to non-existence. And believing in yourself alone, is a lonely existence and is on the same scale.

I, on the other hand, believe in God Almighty, and I also believe in the spiritual universe; because although I believe in God, I do understand that he is a spirit in the spiritual universe. I believe that he has my back, and that he does look after my well-being in the physical universe. Yes, I do pray to God, and that is my communication method between the two universes, and when he wants to communicate back, he will—sometimes through visions.

Yes, I have had visions before. One is to become a role model to sickle cell children, and to teach them how to survive and thrive in this world. I have had other visions, which have changed the way I thought, and my career path.

The key thing is to believe in something or someone who will lift you and carry you along to the place you want to be; and if you stumble or fall, they will be there with you to pick you up. It may just be a coach or a mentor, but you have to make sure that there is somebody that will help you out when you need a hand.

Don't get me wrong; I am not preaching at you. You can be an atheist for all I care, but just recognise that you can't do it all alone. There will come a time when you need help, and that is what is great about having the right mentor or coach. They are there to pick you up when you are struggling.

Faith

'Optimism is the faith that leads to achievement. Nothing can be done without hope and confidence." – **Helen Keller**

Faith is something made by man and is linked to religion. I have an abundance of faith and belief in myself. From an early age, I have always believed in the spiritual being called God, and his son, Jesus Christ, as the one being.

When I was in hospital, I had more faith in this notion, and the belief that with God's help and understanding, and love, I would come out of this transplant fit and well. I would pray to him constantly to help me through the day, to help me conquer the pain, and to help me through the boredom. It was a comfort to know that there was someone out there looking after me at all times.

Faith is said to be in the physical universe, as it is made by man and is something you truly believe in, and it is the true doctrines of a religion based on a spiritual conviction rather than on actual proof. True religious faith helps comfort those who believe in it, to get through their days, one by one.

I have also believed in the Lord God since I was a child, and my faith is something that I really hung onto during the tough times of my transplant procedure, as I prayed to God to get me through the tough parts.

However, that was not the only thing that got me through it all, although, I'd like to say it is. But the other thing that held fast was having a truly positive mindset that I could overcome anything and everything put in front of me. It was just another hurdle to overcome. Having a truly unwavering positive mindset is very useful in going into anything like this; however, there were moments when I needed a little bit extra to carry me forward, and that was when I turned to my faith.

It can be said that I am lucky in a sense, having something to believe in that lifts me and carries me that extra mile, but I don't see that as luck. I really see it as what it is: faith. Whether it is God, or Allah, or Buddha, or something else you believe in, your faith will carry you that extra mile.

And when you combine that with an unstoppable mindset, you can overcome anything.

Spirituality

"More smiling, less worrying. More compassion, less judgement. More blessed, less stressed. More love, less hate." – **Roy T. Bennett**

It is hard not to believe in the spiritual universe. It is all around us. I believe that the Father, Son, and Holy Spirit are all in the spiritual universe, and his son, Jesus, came down to earth as a man, and went back as a spirit.

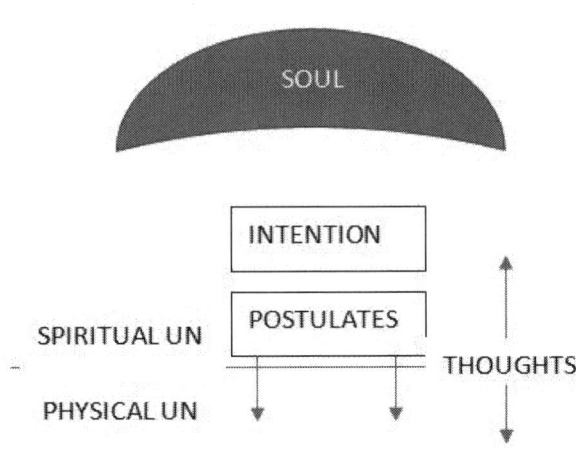

The spiritual universe is also where your soul lives when it is not in you. However, when on earth, it deals with what life gives you, and goes through all challenges with you.

Remember, there is nothing out there, which means that there is nothing out there but the life you create for yourself. You interact with other people by what you create and intercept in their own universe. If this is true, you create your own life, and if you don't like it, you can change it. To do this, you must first start by looking at your intentions and what they are. Come up with six new intentions for your life that are positive and meaningful. Start small, and then grow bigger in time.

These intentions will now be your new driving force and the purpose of your life. They will be what pushes you to succeed or fail in life, so make them strong and positive. Out of those intentions will be a series of thoughts, and these then become postulates.

Postulates are the result of having good intentions, and they will manifest in the physical universe in all kinds of positive ways, like finding a lot of money, finding a way to pay for the thing you always wanted to do, or finding a solution for a problem you so desperately wish to solve. All of these are postulates, and a gift from the universe.

> *"We are not human beings having a spiritual experience. We are spiritual beings having a human experience."*
> *Pierre Teilhard de Chardin*

The spiritual universe is where all good things come from, but it shouldn't be ignored in any way, because it can also punish you if you ignore all good things that it gives you, as it may not give you anything else for a few months.

However, it is great to believe in both the spiritual world and having complete faith in God as well, because believing and understanding both, helps you in so many ways, and helps you focus the mind on things you want to accomplish.

Part 5

My Story Ends ... for Now!

Chapter 9

Positive Mind, Positive Vibes, Positive Life

I think the reason I behave the way I do is because of my upbringing and the experiences I have had throughout my life.

An example of this is that I have only ever had two male role models in my life: my father, the late Admiral Adekunle Lawal, and my Uncle Kinde, both of whom died at an early age. My father died when I was ten years old, and the school I was at advised my mother not to take me out of school for the funeral. I was ten years old, and the eldest male in the family (which was a big deal in African families). This was the first thing in my life that I was told I couldn't do, so I made it known that I was not happy about the decision. I shut down all communication with the school, and went about for several weeks without talking to any teacher.

The next person to die was my uncle, who was there all the time when my mum struggled. He would drive us to places and keep us company, and would always be there in any way he could.

To be honest with you, you never really lose anybody in life. When I struggle in life and need to make a decision, I always think back and ask those two people what they would do in that situation, or picture how they would react, and most of the time, I get the answers I need to move on. I still find myself doing this, twenty-five to thirty-five years later, as it is still a comfort to me to know that they are still there looking out for me and my well-being.

This is a classic example of my constant communication with the spiritual universe, and getting the answers I need back from it, and I don't see a problem with this. I could say that these two people, along with my mother, helped assist in shaping my life and what I am today; and my moral compass was built on the foundations created from the teachings of my mother and father.

Another teaching I got from my mother and father was to stand up for yourself and your beliefs. Never let somebody tell you that you are not capable of doing something. If you think you can do it, and really want to do it, then don't let someone get in your way. It took a while to get this message, but when I did, there was no stopping me. If there was someone I believed could help me achieve something, and they didn't do just that, I dropped them, and found someone else to teach me and help me grow. I wasn't being pushy in any way, just focused.

With all the battles throughout my life, and the challenges I have had during school, university, and work, it has framed me to become who I am now. I have helped hundreds of people turn their careers around or develop new careers, with all kinds of training techniques and topics. However, now I have developed new courses, and I teach the "why," and the ultimate mindset for success. All I want to do is see people reach their maximum success in life, whatever that may be.

I have learnt a lot on this journey, which has enabled me to improve my financial situation and business situation with the vast knowledge I have learnt, and I want to help others do the same.

Living Pain-Free

I can't tell you how good it really feels to be pain-free for the first time in my life that I can remember. For the first month or two out of hospital, I was so confused; I kept on waking up expecting to have some niggling pain, or expecting it to come up throughout the day. However... Nothing! No pain.

I even did a walk after a few days of being home, only to find that I had done 10 km, all terrain walking, and I didn't feel anything. This was quite astonishing. So I told the doctor, and she said,"Well, we don't normally advise our patients to do that, but in your case..." Then she shrugged her shoulders.

This was my determination and mindset going on over-drive. This was a weird feeling for me. I felt that I could accomplish anything. The stronger I got, and the sharper my mind got, I decided to come to grips with my businesses and go back to work after a few months.

I also found that I could do things now that I could never do before because I had sickle cell anaemia. I found that I could do more in the gym, my treks were longer, I have more stamina, and I have overcome more challenges.

It has been two and a half years since the transplant, and I have never felt better. However, I still need the all-clear from the doctors, but they are hesitating for some reason. Either way, I will keep going on, and keep helping others.

Gratitude

As I have mentioned previously, I feel extremely blessed and extremely grateful for what I have achieved in my life, but most of all in the past five years.

If it weren't for my family, I wouldn't have got to where I am today; and if it weren't for my wife and her persistence and wisdom, we wouldn't have been able to raise the funds as quickly as we did. She made a lot of effort to keep me cheerful and entertained throughout my strokes, my rehab, and my stem cell transplant. She is truly a gift from the heavens, sent to look after my well-being. For this, I am truly thankful.

As for my brother, Gbenga, what can I say about him? You couldn't ask for a better person in your life. For someone to voluntarily stand up and be counted, and donate his stem cells to another human, yet alone his elder brother, is truly an amazing thing. Saying thank you to him is not enough. He is an angel.

I am also grateful to the nurses and doctors that took their time to look after me and to make sure that I was fit and well, and cared for me throughout the last five years.

I feel extremely grateful for the second chance I have in life, and I have a deep respect for anyone who has to go through such gruelling treatments, like having their immune systems reset by drugs like Campath, or by radiotherapy. I also have respect for all the sickle cell sufferers out there, and it is my mission to one day help them in any way I can, through my foundation.

It is also my mission to help people rebuild their mindset for success in life, and to help individuals realise their "why" in business, to overcome obstacles and reach success in anything they choose to do. This is because I have been blessed with learning these techniques and the knowledge, and I wish to help others by sharing it.

Here and Now

My stubborn tenacity has kept me going. I am now travelling around Europe helping people, and at the moment, I am sitting in a hotel in Dunboyne, County Meath, Ireland, writing this final part of the book. I am here working for a very unique pharmaceutical company that specialises in rare diseases, and makes drugs to help cure or aid people with those diseases.

My doctors are not willing to give me the all-clear yet, but they are starting to look optimistic. I am almost off the main immune-suppression drugs, and I feel great—so great, I could conquer the world.

Remember:

"You never know how strong you are, until being strong is the only choice you have."– Bob Marley

And

"Train your mind to be calm in every situation."
– Unknown Author

Part 6

A Medical Overview

This part of the book is here to provide a brief medical overview of sickle cell anaemia, strokes, and stem cell transfers. I have included this information as reference material, just in case you are unfamiliar with any of the conditions or procedures that I went through, and want more information.

Chapter 10

Sickle Cell

What Is It?

Sickle cell disease is a group of disorders that affects the haemoglobin, the molecule in the red blood cells throughout the body. People with this disorder have atypical haemoglobin molecules called haemoglobin S, which can distort the red blood cells into a sickle shape or crescent shape.

The signs and symptoms usually begin when the person with the disease is in his/her childhood, and the severity of the symptoms usually vary from one individual to another. Some people are affected with mild symptoms, while others are frequently hospitalised with more serious complications.

Sickle cell disease affects millions of people around the world: most commonly found in people whose ancestors are from Africa; Mediterranean countries, such as Greece, Turkey, and Italy; the Arabian Peninsula; India; Spanish speaking regions, like South and Central America; and parts of the Caribbean. In recent times of travel and migration, even some American and English citizens have sickle cell.

Sickle cell is the most common inherited blood disorder in the United States and United Kingdom, affecting 70,000 to 80,000 Americans, and 12,500 to 15,000 British people. The disease affects 1 in 500 Black Americans, and 1 in 1,400 Hispanic Americans.

How Does Sickle Cell Disease Affect the Blood?

Sickle cell disease affects the haemoglobin in the red blood cells. It very often changes the shape of the blood cells, and this can cause pain and other problems.

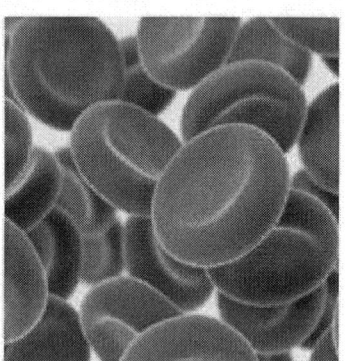

Normal Red Blood Cell Flow

Red Blood Cells

Your blood is made up of several different components. Each does a different job. The main parts are:

- **Plasma** is the liquid part of blood, which carries all other components around the body to where they are needed.

- **White blood cells** help to destroy bacteria and infections, and help heal cuts and injuries that occur.

- **Red blood cells** make the blood look red, and they are normally a round disc shape. They carry oxygen around the body, from the lungs, in a substance called haemoglobin. Sickle cell disease affects the red blood cells.

- **Platelets** help the blood to clot if people cut themselves.

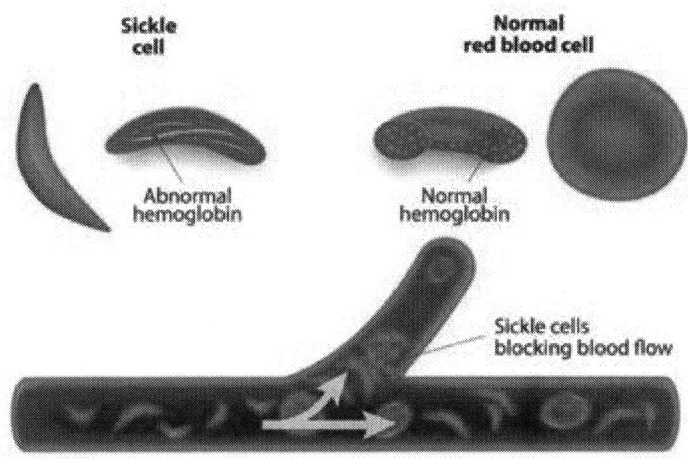

Sickle Cell Blood Flow

Haemoglobin is the substance in the red blood cells that carries oxygen. The red blood cells pick up the oxygen in the lungs, and carries it around the body. It then delivers the oxygen to wherever it is needed.

There are approximately 300 different kinds of haemoglobin, the most common being haemoglobin A (The A stands for adult.). The kinds that are most important, when looking at sickle cell disease, are *sickle haemoglobin* and *haemoglobin C*. Thalassaemia, a condition in which the body cannot produce enough haemoglobin, is also important.

The type of haemoglobin anyone has, depends on what they inherit from both parents. Most people inherit haemoglobin A. Some people inherit other kinds.

If both parents have haemoglobin AS (which means they are a carrier of sickle cell but don't have the full disease), there is a one-in-four chance that they will have a child with haemoglobin SS (which is full-blown sickle cell anaemia.)

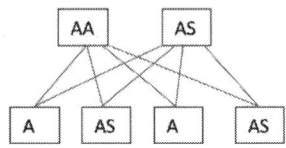

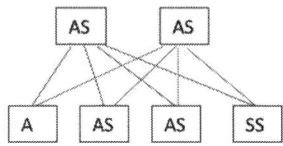

One Parent carrier will product on Child carrier in four   Both Parent carriers will product on Sickle Cell Child in four

How can it affect you?

Acute painful sickle cell episode (also known as painful crisis) is an acute condition that occurs in people with sickle cell disease. In these people, red blood cells behave differently under a variety of conditions, including dehydration, low oxygen levels, and elevated temperature. Changes in any of these conditions may cause the red blood cells to block the small blood vessels, restricting blood flow. This damages the tissue, which causes pain.

Having full-blown sickle cell anaemia, where you have a Haemoglobin type SS, can manifest its crisis and surrounding illnesses in different ways. The disease can cause liver damage, respiratory difficulties, organ failure, hypertension, and other chronic diseases to happen in your body.

Most commonly, it can create a crisis in your body, which is where the cells, shaped like a sickle, get caught up amongst other similar cells and block the arteries or veins. This is called a blood clot, and with sickle cell, it can happen anywhere in the body, at any time of the day. Most of these happen in the arms or legs (in my case), but they can happen in other areas as well.

It has been said, many times, by people that are having a crisis, that it is like being hit by two double-decker buses, and being squashed like a sandwich filling. The pain you get is so intense, all you want is to be given a hard-core painkiller, like morphine or pethidine, or something in that drug family. In fact, when you go to hospital, that is the first thing they give you, followed by a lot of fluids, and this is repeated continuously for between three and seven days, until the pain goes away, when the blood clot eases.

I have had three occasions where I have had blood clots in my lungs, leading to pulmonary embolisms and pneumonia. This left scar tissue in my lungs, and for years I would get one or two chest infections every year. This was no fun at all.

Some of the causes of a crisis include:

1. **Reduced supply of oxygen** to various parts of the body. For example, strenuous exercise. Normal exercise is all right; however, too much may cause sickling. Each person knows what level of exercise they can handle.

2. **Dehydration**, which is too little liquid in the body. This can happen if a person does not drink enough liquid, or they have become hot and have perspired a lot during exercise, or because of vomiting or diarrhoea.

3. **Infection.** For example, a chest infection or pneumonia.

4. **Anaesthetics**, which are gases or drugs used before an operation to put people asleep. Anaesthetics can be dangerous to a person with sickle cell disease because they may cause sickling due to lack of oxygen, and dehydration. Doctors must take care to prevent sickling. If you have to have anaesthetic, you must inform the doctor if you have sickle cell disease, and try to find other alternatives. For small operations, try to get them to do this under

local anaesthetic. This would put the body under far less stress, and they can monitor you closely.

5. **Sudden changes of temperature**, such as going from a warm room to a cold place.

6. **Alcohol**. This may lead to a crisis by causing dehydration.

7. **Emotional Stress**, such as feeling under pressure, or being depressed.

It is important to know the things that may cause sickling, so that you can avoid them as much as possible. However, sickling can happen without any of these symptoms, and without anybody knowing why. One of the most common problems is caused by the actual sickling pain itself.

How Is Sickle Cell Disease Inherited?

Genes come in pairs. You inherit 1 set from your mother and 1 set from your father.

To be born with sickle cell disease, a child has to inherit a copy of the sickle cell gene from both their parents.

This usually happens when both parents are "carriers" of the sickle cell gene, also known as having the sickle cell trait.

Or it can happen when 1 parent has sickle cell disease, and the other is a carrier of it.

Sickle cell carriers do not have sickle cell disease themselves, but there's a chance they could have a child with sickle cell disease if their partner is also a carrier.

If both parents are sickle cell carriers, there's a:

- 1 in 4 chance that each child they have will not inherit any sickle cell genes, and will not have sickle cell disease or be able to pass it on.

- 1 in 2 chance that each child they have will just inherit a copy of the sickle cell gene from 1 parent, and be a carrier.

- 1 in 4 chance that each child they have will inherit copies of the sickle cell gene from both parents, and will be born with sickle cell disease.

The Sickle Cell Society has more information about the inheritance of sickle cell disease, including what the risks are if a parent has sickle cell disease themselves.

Chapter 11

Strokes

What Are Strokes?

It can be said that a stroke is a medical condition brought on by poor blood flow to the brain, which results in dead cells. There are two main types of stokes you can get: ischemic, due to a lack of blood flow, and haemorrhagic, due to bleeding. Both types result in the brain function not operating fully.

The signs and symptoms of a stroke may include an inability to move (known as hemiparesis) or to feel on one side of the body, problems understanding or speaking (such as your words and speech becoming slurred), dizziness, or loss of vision on one side. Signs and symptoms often appear soon after the stroke has occurred. If symptoms last less than one or two hours, it is known as a transient ischemic attack (TIA), or mini-stroke. The symptoms of a stroke can be permanent. Long-term complications may include pneumonia or loss of bladder control.

The main risk factor for stroke is high blood pressure (hypertension). Other risk factors include tobacco smoking, obesity, high blood cholesterol, diabetes mellitus, a previous TIA, and atrial fibrillation. An ischemic stroke is typically caused by blockage of a blood vessel, though there are also less common causes. (Unfortunately, this was the cause of my strokes, due to a crisis/clot in the brain.)

Diagnosis is typically based on a physical examination, and generally supported by medical imaging such as a CT scan (**computed tomography scan,** formerly **computerized axial tomography scan** or **CAT scan**), which makes use of computer-processed combinations of many x-ray measurements, taken from different angles, to produce cross-sectional (tomographic) images, or an MRI scan. **Magnetic resonance imaging (MRI)** is a medical imaging technique used in radiology to form pictures of the anatomy and the physiological processes of the body. MRI scanners use strong magnetic fields, magnetic field gradients, and radio waves to generate images of the organs in the body. A CT scan can rule out bleeding but may not necessarily rule out ischemia, which typically does not show up on a CT scan early on. Other tests, such as an electrocardiogram (ECG) and blood tests, are done to determine risk factors and to rule out other possible causes.

Knowing your stroke risk factors, following your doctor's recommendations, and adopting a healthy lifestyle are the best steps you can take to prevent a stroke. If you've had a stroke or a transient ischemic attack (TIA), these measures might help prevent another stroke. The follow-up care you receive in the hospital and afterwards may play a role as well.

Many stroke prevention strategies are the same as the strategies to prevent heart disease. In general, healthy lifestyle recommendations include:

Controlling high blood pressure (hypertension). This is one of the most important things you can do to reduce your stroke risk. If you've had a stroke, lowering your blood pressure can help prevent a subsequent TIA or stroke.

Exercising, managing stress, maintaining a healthy weight, and limiting the amount of sodium and alcohol you eat and drink can all help to keep high blood pressure in check. In addition to recommending lifestyle changes, your doctor may prescribe medications to treat high blood pressure.

Lowering the amount of cholesterol and saturated fat in your diet. Eating less cholesterol and fat, especially saturated fat and trans fats, may reduce the plaque in your arteries. If you can't control your cholesterol through dietary changes alone, your doctor may prescribe a cholesterol-lowering medication.

Quitting tobacco use. Smoking raises the risk of stroke, for smokers and non-smokers, who are exposed to second-hand smoke. Quitting tobacco use reduces your risk of stroke.

Controlling diabetes. You can manage diabetes with diet, exercise, weight control, and medication.

Maintaining a healthy weight. Being overweight contributes to other stroke risk factors, such as high blood pressure, cardiovascular disease, and diabetes. Losing as little as 10 pounds may lower your blood pressure and improve your cholesterol levels.

Eating a diet rich in fruits and vegetables. A diet containing five or more daily servings of fruits or vegetables may reduce your risk of stroke. Following the Mediterranean diet, which emphasizes olive oil, fruit, nuts, vegetables, and whole grains, may be helpful.

Exercising regularly. Aerobic or *cardio* exercise reduces your risk of stroke in many ways. Exercise can lower your blood pressure, increase your level of high-density lipoprotein cholesterol, and improve the overall health of your blood vessels and heart. It also helps you lose weight, control diabetes, and reduce stress. Gradually work up to 30 minutes of activity—such as walking, jogging, swimming, or bicycling— on most, if not all, days of the week.

Drinking alcohol in moderation, if at all. Alcohol can be both a risk factor and a protective measure for stroke. Heavy alcohol consumption increases your risk of high blood pressure, ischemic strokes, and haemorrhagic strokes. However, drinking small to moderate amounts of alcohol, such as one drink a day, may help prevent ischemic stroke, and decrease your blood's clotting tendency. Alcohol may also interact with other drugs you're taking. Talk to your doctor about what's appropriate for you.

Treating obstructive sleep apnoea (OSA). Your doctor may recommend an overnight oxygen assessment to screen for OSA—a sleep disorder in which the oxygen level intermittently drops during the night. Treatment for OSA includes oxygen at night or wearing a small device in your mouth to help you breathe.

Avoiding illegal drugs. Certain street drugs, such as cocaine and methamphetamines, are established risk factors for a TIA or a stroke. Cocaine reduces blood flow and can narrow the arteries.

Chapter 12

Stem Cell Transplant for Sickle Cell

Why This Stem Cell Transplant Study?

This SCT study is for those diagnosed with a severe congenital anaemia in which allogeneic bone marrow transplantation has been shown to be potentially curative. Patients with severe congenital anaemias, such as sickle cell disease and β-thalassemia, have been successfully transplanted and cured. However, treatment has been limited to those who are younger than the age of 18, as it is known that younger patients tolerate transplant better than older patients. Safer procedures for performing allogeneic transplantation have evolved over the last decade, and suggest that age may no longer be a reason not to consider this potentially curative procedure.

Transplantation is complicated, but it is hoped that the information provided here is clear enough to help people decide two very important things: firstly, whether a research transplant seems the right choice, and secondly, whether you wish to accept the experimental research protocol that is being offered. You should also discuss all possible treatment options with your doctor before making a decision about the NIH experimental transplant protocol. In particular, patients with sickle cell disease need to have tried hydroxyurea, unless they have had an irreversible complication such as a stroke, kidney damage, or liver damage, as hydroxyurea has been shown to improve life expectancy in most patients with sickle cell disease.

You are eligible to participate in this study because:

- you have a family member who is a suitable tissue match,
- your pre-transplant evaluations and blood tests are consistent with protocol entry requirements, and
- you are not pregnant (subjects must avoid pregnancy while in the study due to the risk of harming the baby).

The National Institute of Health plan to enrol a maximum of 50 bone marrow recipients in this study.

They did just that to start with, and then increased the numbers to suit as they allocated their research funds to improve the risk of half matched siblings from 10 percent to a much greater figure.

All I can say is that this was a very honourable piece of research that worked for me, and I would like to thank Dr. Tisdale and his team for creating this procedure.

What Is an Allogeneic Stem Cell Transplant?

Allogeneic (using cells from a healthy donor) Research Stem Cell Transplantation is capable of curing a number of different blood diseases, including leukaemia and lymphoma, as well as some congenital anaemias. Stem cell transplant involves the use of high intensity treatment with chemotherapy and often radiation to the bone marrow and the rest of the body to destroy all of the abnormal cells. This is the reason for giving back your donor's normal marrow cells, including bone marrow stem cells, after chemotherapy. The **donor cells (graft)** find their way to the bone marrow, where they generate normally functioning blood cells for the rest of your life. In addition, immune cells from the donor generate a new immune system to help fight infection. Of equal importance is the strong immune attack made by the donor's immune cells against any residual abnormal bone marrow cells left in your body after the chemotherapy. This is called graft versus marrow (GVM) effect. This is because donor immune cells are capable of recognizing patients' cells as being foreign, and destroying them.

How does this research stem cell transplant differ from a standard stem cell transplant?

This transplant differs from a standard transplant because it does not contain any chemotherapy at all. Standard transplants generally use a high dose of radiation in combination with a chemotherapeutic drug. Given that many patients with anaemias, especially those with sickle cell disease, will already have some kidney damage, we would like to avoid the use of any drugs, which rely on the kidney to be eliminated or which can cause more damage to the kidney. Furthermore, most patients with sickle cell disease, and all patients with β-thalassemia, will have received a number of red blood cell transfusions, which can make accepting a graft more difficult. Instead, we will use a relatively low dose of radiation (300 rad), which is about one-third the dose that is traditionally used in standard allogeneic BMT (anywhere from 1000–1300rad). It will be combined with two immunosuppressive drugs to help prevent your body from rejecting your donor's cells. With this dose of irradiation and no standard chemotherapeutic agent, this regimen may prove to be even less toxic and more effective for patients with congenital anaemias.

The risk of using such a non-toxic regimen is that it is more likely for the transplant to fail, and for you to reject the graft. However, with this modified approach, unlike with standard BMT, if your graft should fail, your own bone marrow will eventually recover. Previously, if the graft failed, the patient could not survive, but this is not the case with using a more modified treatment. Of course, if the graft did fail, that would mean that you would not be cured, but for some patients with sickle cell disease (one of the diseases included under the heading of severe congenital anaemia), in whom this has happened, their sickle cell disease became less severe for at least a couple of years after the transplant procedure. This is not true if you have a different kind of anaemia. The other risk is that by using drugs that are not chemotherapeutic but more immunosuppressive, you will be at higher risk of developing infections after receiving these drugs. This can occur whether the transplant does or does not succeed. For this reason, even if the transplant does not work, we will need to monitor you for at least 6 months to watch for any signs of infections. We currently have several protocols under study in a variety of patients at high risk for complications with standard BMT using other modified forms of transplant, and our preliminary results are encouraging. The experimental approaches we are evaluating here are:

1.   Using a low intensity radiation based conditioning regimen, which we call a non-myeloablative approach, which does not completely destroy your marrow, and makes the transplant easier and safer.

2.   Using Sirolimus instead of the standard drug, cyclosporine, to prevent the occurrence of graft versus host disease (GVHD).

These features are described in detail below. The protocol does not differ in other important details from other nonmyeloablative (bone marrow sparing) protocols being developed around the country.

The Protocol – How Is It Done?

Your pre-transplantation evaluation

You and your donor will visit our outpatient clinic at the National Institutes of Health Clinical Center, and have full medical histories taken, physical examinations performed, and about 6 tablespoons of blood drawn. This blood will be used to confirm your diagnosis, to check whether or not you have had exposures to a number of common viruses, and to make sure that your liver and kidney function is good enough for transplantation. We will repeat the compatibility testing (HLA testing) between you and your donor, even if your typing was done elsewhere, to make sure that the two of you are a very good match.

You will have breathing tests, and tests of heart function, and you may have x-rays of your chest, abdomen, and sinuses, to make sure that these organs are in good shape for transplantation. You will also undergo bone marrow sampling, with withdrawal of approximately a tablespoon of marrow from your pelvic bone in order to collect samples to confirm the present state of your blood condition, and for research purposes. You will have your teeth and eyes checked, and any problems treated that could cause complications during the transplant. You will also see an endocrine doctor to assess fertility and glands, such as your thyroid. We will ask you questions about your fertility health so that we can learn how the transplant process affects fertility. In addition, you will participate in neuropsychological testing so that we can assess how the transplant process affects your cognitive functioning (e.g., attention, memory, and problem solving), emotional functioning (e.g., depression, anxiety), and quality of life (e.g., everyday behaviour).

Line Placement

Prior to your transplant, it will be arranged for a placement of a large intravenous line (like a Hickman line) that can stay in your body for the entire duration of transplant and recovery period. This will be your "lifeline" for transfusions of red cells and platelets, antibiotics, intravenous feeding, and other intravenous medications, and will even be used to give you the blood stem cells from your donor. This line can also be used for blood drawing, avoiding almost all needle sticks during the transplant and recovery period. The line is put in under local or, rarely, general anaesthesia, in the radiology department or, even more rarely, the operating room. It enters the body in the upper part of the chest, and is then tunnelled under the skin to feed into a vein in the chest or neck. You may feel some discomfort and stiffness in your chest and shoulder for a few days after the line has been placed.

The risks from the procedure are low: light-headedness or, rarely, fainting due to the temporary lowering of blood pressure; bleeding, bruising, or infection at the site of insertion. Very rarely, there may be collapse of one lung during line insertion. If the lung collapses, a tube may have to be inserted through the skin into the chest, and remain in place until the lung re-expands. Because of this, you will have a chest x-ray following the procedure, to make sure that the line is in the correct place and that the lung is not collapsed. We will leave the line in for as long as necessary, which may be up to 3–6 months. If the line becomes clogged or infected, it would have to be replaced by a new line. The line will need to be flushed once a day to try and prevent clogging.

References

NHS Website:
https://www.nhs.uk/conditions/sickle-cell-disease
Clinical Research Study by Dr. John F. Tisdale
Sickle Cell Society
www.sicklecellsociety.org